Presented to

Charlie Shelton

Easter Sunday

March 23, 2008

By Grandma & Grandpa Shelton

We love you very much & Know that God will watch over you & direct you down the BEST path!

Proverbs 3:5-6

This book is a celebration of Jesus Christ, God's perfect gift. He is the full and complete image of the Father's love—its breadth, length, depth, and height. The life of Jesus is the expression of God's heart to you. He came for you, lived for you, died for you, and rose from the dead for you. He is the One your eyes can look to . . . your faith can lean upon . . . and your life can depend upon. Jesus Christ is the love that your heart can daily come to know. As you think upon all He's done for you, may you become all that His love created you to be.

Roy Lessin

GOD SENT US A SAVIOR

A Collection by Roy Lessin

Paintings by Chris Hopkins

Chariot Victor Publishing
Cook Communications, Colorado Springs, CO 80918
Cook Communications, Paris, Ontario
Kingsway Communications, Eastbourne, England

Design: Bill Gray
Editor: Julie Smith
Interior Design: Cheryl Ogletree
First printing, 1998
Printed in the United States of America
1 2 3 4 5 6 7 8 9 10 Printing/Year 02 01 00 99 98

Library of Congress Cataloging-in-Publication Data

God sent us a Savior: a collection/[written by] Roy Lessin.
p. cm.
ISBN 1-56476-735-3
1. Jesus Christ--Biography--Devotional literature. I. Lessin, Roy.
BT306.5.G63 1998
232.9'01--dc21
[B] 98-17288
CIP

FROM

ON

CONTENTS

HE CAME IN A WAY THAT FULFILLED SO MUCH 8

HE LIVED IN A WAY THAT GAVE SO MUCH 24

HE LOVED IN A WAY THAT MEANS SO MUCH 36

HE ROSE IN A WAY THAT CONQUERED SO MUCH 48

HE CAME IN A WAY THAT FULFILLED SO MUCH

He Came

In those days Caesar Augustus issued a decree that a census should be taken of the entire Roman world. . . . And everyone went to his own town to register.

So Joseph also went up from the town of Nazareth in Galilee to Judea, to Bethlehem the town of David, because he belonged to the house and line of David. He went there to register with Mary, who was pledged to be married to him and was expecting a child. While they were there, the time came for the baby to be born, and she gave birth to her firstborn, a son. She wrapped him in cloths and placed him in a manger, because there was no room for them in the inn.

And there were shepherds living out in the fields nearby, keeping watch over their flocks at night. An angel of the Lord appeared to them, and the glory of the Lord shone around them, and they were terrified. But the angel said to them, "Do not be afraid. I bring you good news of great joy that will be for all the people. Today in the town of David a Savior has been born to you; he is Christ the Lord. This will be a sign to you: you will find a baby wrapped in cloths and lying in a manger."

Suddenly a great company of the heavenly host appeared with the angel, praising God and saying,

> "Glory to God in the highest,
> and on earth peace to men on whom his favor rests."

When the angels had left them and gone into heaven, the shepherds said to one another, "Let's go to Bethlehem and see this thing that has happened, which the Lord has told us about."

So they hurried off and found Mary and Joseph, and the baby, who was lying in the manger. When they had seen him, they spread the word concerning what had been told them about this child, and all who heard it were amazed at what the shepherds said to them. But Mary treasured up all these things and pondered them in her heart. The shepherds returned, glorifying and praising God for all the things they had heard and seen, which were just as they had been told.

Luke 2:1-20

GOD SENT US A SAVIOR

If our greatest need had been information,
God would have sent us an educator.
If our greatest need had been technology,
God would have sent us a scientist.
If our greatest need had been money,
God would have sent us an economist.
If our greatest need had been pleasure,
God would have sent us an entertainer.
But our greatest need was forgiveness,
So God sent us a Savior.

And she shall bring forth a son, and thou shalt call his name Jesus: for he shall save his people from their sins.

Matthew 1:21 (KJV)

URPOSE

Purpose to seek Him—He will be your reward.

Purpose to know Him—He will reveal Himself to you.

Purpose to follow Him—He will lead the way.

Purpose to enjoy Him—He will be your dearest friend.

Purpose to praise Him—He will be your song.

Purpose to trust Him—He will be your provider.

Purpose to please Him—He will not keep
anything good from you.

Purpose to be totally His—He will be totally yours!

When you get right down to it . . .
the only thing that really matters is Jesus!

Daily, through books, movies, radio, television, and conversation, we are told by the world what we need in our lives to be fulfilled and happy. We hear about the value of education, the pleasures of entertainment, the necessity of finances, and the importance of technology. But when it comes to the thing we need the most, the world is silent. God, through Christ, has made our greatest need known—it is our need of forgiveness and a new life in Him.

He Came

"Come, all you who are thirsty,

come to the waters;

and you who have no money,

come, buy and eat!

Come, buy wine and milk

without money and without cost.

Why spend money on what is not bread,

and your labor on what does not satisfy?

Listen, listen to me, and eat what is good,

and your soul will delight in the richest of fare.

Give ear and come to me;

hear me, that your soul may live.

I will make an everlasting covenant with you,

my faithful love promised to David,"

declares the Lord.

Isaiah 55:1-3

The gift that God gave to us

is for our hearts to hold.

It can't be bought with precious jewels,

or with the finest gold.

The gift that God gave to us

is free in every way;

for the price of our salvation

is the one we could not pay.

The gift that God gave to us

is Jesus Christ His Son;

worthy of our life and love,

given for everyone.

JESUS THE FAITHFUL ONE

The confidence we have . . . the trust we hold . . .

the hope we carry . . . rest in His faithfulness.

Every promise He has made He purposes to fulfill.

He has the authority to accomplish all He has spoken.

His power is limitless . . . His character changeless . . .

His love endless.

The Savior's coming means you can trust the One who is faithful to His Word to fulfill every promise He has spoken to you through His Son.

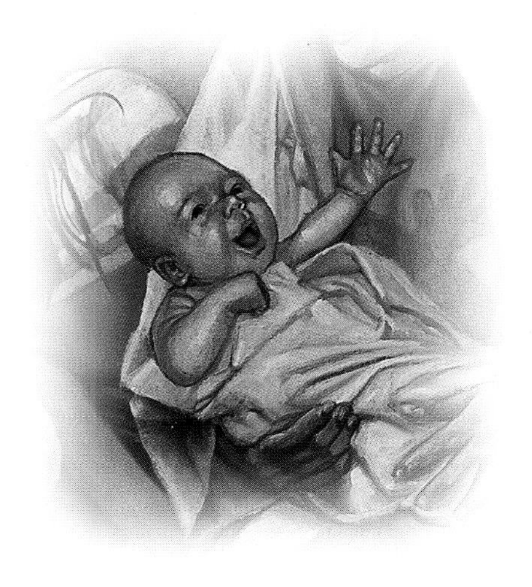

The coming of the Savior is a celebration of the faithfulness of God. Every prophecy that God spoke concerning the coming of the Messiah as our Redeemer was fulfilled by Jesus Christ.

His humble virgin birth in the town of Bethlehem, His journey into Egypt, His maturing years in Nazareth, His holy and blameless life, His suffering and death on the cross, and His triumphant Resurrection—all were a part of the prophecies that He fulfilled.

JESUS THE WONDERFUL ONE

He is greater than any ruler,

Mightier than any warrior,

Nobler than any king,

Wiser than any sage,

Greater than any kingdom,

Lovelier than any crown,

Higher than any name.

No one could be more worthy of our worship,

our love, and our life-long devotion.

THE GREATEST GIFT

Have you ever wondered why God announced the greatest birth in human history to a handful of shepherds on a hillside and a few wise men from the East?

Perhaps it was because they were quiet enough to listen, eager enough to know, and available enough to follow!

The seeking heart finds at journey's end,
Jesus as its closest friend!

He Came

Where would we be without Jesus?

He was born of a woman so that we could be born of God . . .

He humbled Himself so we could be lifted up . . .

He became a servant so we could be made heirs . . .

He suffered rejection so we could become His friends . . .

He denied Himself so we could freely receive all things.

God's love gift—

Mary nurtured Him,

Joseph provided for Him,

Angels ministered to Him,

Disciples followed Him,

Man crucified Him,

The Holy Spirit raised Him,

God exalted Him,

Hearts receive Him,

Voices praise Him,

Lives glorify Him,

Worshipers adore Him.

He Came

Although times have changed,

our needs remain the same . . .

and love that was in Jesus

and the life He gave 2,000 years ago

are present today to bring

joy to your world . . .

purpose to your life . . .

and love to your heart.

As we look back and rejoice in what Christ did for us through the humility of His birth and death—think of what our joy will be like when we see Him coming in all His power and glory!

We who had so little have received so much, because He has given so freely!

HE LIVED IN A WAY THAT GAVE SO MUCH

One day as he was teaching, Pharisees and teachers of the law, who had come from every village of Galilee and from Judea and Jerusalem, were sitting there. And the power of the Lord was present for him to heal the sick. Some men came carrying a paralytic on a mat and tried to take him into the house to lay him before Jesus. When they could not find a way to do this because of the crowd, they went up on the roof and lowered him on his mat through the tiles into the middle of the crowd, right in front of Jesus.

When Jesus saw their faith, he said, "Friend, your sins are forgiven."

The Pharisees and the teachers of the law began thinking to themselves, "Who is this fellow who speaks blasphemy? Who can forgive sins but God alone?"

Jesus knew what they were thinking and asked, "Why are you thinking these things in your hearts? Which is easier: to say, 'Your sins are forgiven,' or to say, 'Get up and walk'? But that you may know that the Son of Man has authority on earth to forgive sins. . . ." He said to the paralyzed man, "I tell you, get up, take your mat and go home." Immediately he stood up in front of them, took what he had been lying on and went home praising God. Everyone was amazed and gave praise to God. They were filled with awe and said, "We have seen remarkable things today."

Luke 5:17-26

He came in a way that fulfilled so much . . .

Spoke in a way that taught so much . . .

Died in a way that provided so much . . .

Rose in a way that conquered so much . . .

Lives in a way that gives so much . . .

Loves in a way that means so much.

COME LET US ADORE HIM!

There are no greater riches than those

that are found in the treasure of Jesus Christ—

No deeper joy than the one

that is found in His presence . . .

No sweeter song than the melody

of His love filling the heart . . .

No truer friendship than the one

which comes by walking with Him . . .

No higher calling than to follow

the King of kings and Lord of lords.

Behold Him—

In His eyes the light of life . . .

In His voice the Word of truth . . .

In His feet the steps of peace . . .

In His hands the kingdom's work . . .

In His ears the Spirit's voice . . .

In His heart the Father's love.

He Lived

Teachers can point us to knowledge,

Doctors to medicine,

Theologians to religion,

Philosophers to viewpoints,

But God points us to Jesus—

because all that God is,

and all that we need,

are found in the person of His Son.

In Him we find forgiveness for our sins,

comfort for our sorrows,

healing for our pain,

hope for our despair,

joy for our heaviness,

and love for our emptiness.

The Spirit of the Sovereign Lord is on me,
because the Lord has anointed me
to preach good news to the poor.
He has sent me to bind up the brokenhearted,
to proclaim freedom for the captives
and release for the prisoners,
to proclaim the year of the Lord's favor
and the day of vengeance of our God,
to comfort all who mourn,
and provide for those who grieve in Zion—
to bestow on them a crown of beauty instead of ashes,
the oil of gladness instead of mourning,
and a garment of praise instead of a spirit of despair.

Isaiah 61:1-3

Jesus replied, ". . . I tell you the truth, if you have faith as small as a mustard seed, you can say to this mountain, 'Move from here to there' and it will move. Nothing will be impossible for you."

Matthew 17:20

Faith is the assurance that regardless

of where you are, what you are doing,

or what you are going through . . .

in all things and in all ways,

God is doing, and will do

the most loving thing concerning you.

God's love gift cannot be purchased in

a store or ordered in a catalog.

It can't be wrapped in a pretty package

with a fancy bow.

But it can be seen in the eyes of a child,

heard in the words of kindness,

and felt in the actions of a friend.

JESUS—THE HEALER

The One who made you knows how to mend you.

He is the Great Physician—

the only One who can heal body, soul, and spirit.

His appointment calendar is never too full . . .

His schedule is never too busy . . .

His diagnosis is accurate . . .

His treatment is gentle . . .

His bedside manner is assuring . . .

His results are wonderful!

You couldn't be in better hands.

JESUS, GOD'S HAND EXTENDED
The hand of the Lord—
extended to empower . . .
bless . . . anoint.
Assuring us of His presence . . .
Enabling us with His grace . . .
Covering us with His glory.
Keeping us safe . . .
Making us whole . . .
Lifting us up.
Touching every aspect
of our lives . . .
Leaving fingerprints of love.

He loved in a way that means so much

People were also bringing babies to Jesus to have him touch them. When the disciples saw this, they rebuked them. But Jesus called the children to him and said, "Let the little children come to me, and do not hinder them, for the kingdom of God belongs to such as these. I tell you the truth, anyone who will not receive the kingdom of God like a little child will never enter it."

Luke 18:15-17

The Word did not become a

philosophy, a theory, or a concept

to be discussed, debated, or argued—

the Word became a Person,

to be followed, enjoyed, and loved.

He reaches out to touch the child,

to hold the weak,

to free the captive,

to embrace the lonely,

to restore all who have wandered away.

His Hands—

Healed the sick so we could know His compassion,

Held a child so we could know His kindness,

Touched the oppressed so we could know His concern,

Bore two spikes so we could know His love!

Those loving hands hold and embrace you today

so that He can keep you close to His heart forever.

Jesus said, "I assure you, unless you turn from your sins and become as little children, you will never get into the Kingdom of Heaven. Therefore, anyone who becomes as humble as this little child is the greatest in the Kingdom of Heaven. And anyone who welcomes a little child like this on my behalf is welcoming me. But if anyone causes one of these little ones who trusts in me to lose faith, it would be better for that person to be thrown into the sea with a large millstone tied around the neck."

Matthew 18:3-6 (NLT)

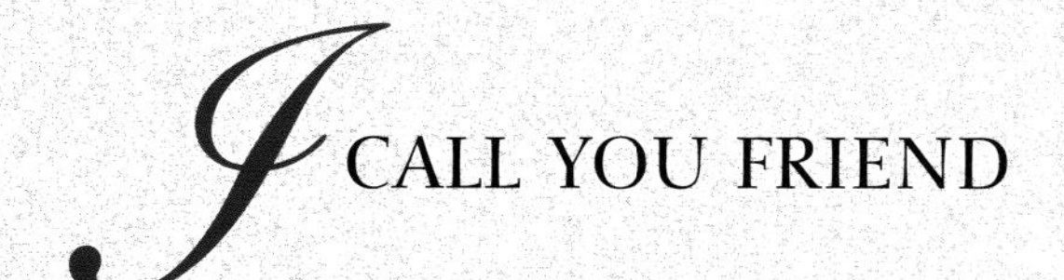

I CALL YOU FRIEND

A stranger may walk behind you,

but I am your friend and walk beside you.

A stranger may be unfamiliar with your ways,

but I am your friend and know your heart.

A stranger may be indifferent to your needs,

but I am your friend and care about you.

A stranger may not know how you feel,

but I am your friend and

share your joy and your pain.

A stranger may keep things from you,

but I am your friend and freely give you My love.

The Child lying in a manger

was God come in the flesh . . .

He was the Lamb of God

come to be the sacrifice for sin . . .

He was the Only Begotten Son

come to reveal the Father's love . . .

He was the King of kings and

Lord of lords come to destroy

the works of Satan. . . .

NO GREATER LOVE

To every child, and every trusting heart,

Jesus reaches out to us in love—

as our Redeemer so He can free us . . .

as our Shepherd so He can care for us . . .

as our Guide so He can lead us . . .

as our Counselor so He can instruct us . . .

as our Lord so He can protect us . . .

as our Friend so He can be with us . . . forever!

HIS WAYS

His ways are good—

they will bring joy to you.

His ways are right—

they will bring wisdom to you.

His ways are true—

they will bring liberty to you.

His ways are pure—

they will bring refreshing to you.

His ways are sure—

they will bring strength to you.

His ways are best—

they will bring blessings to you.

To know Him

you must receive Him like a child . . .

to know His ways

you must trust Him like a child . . .

and like a child,

you will discover His beauty and

the wonder of His ways.

He rose in a way that conquered so much

He Rose

They [the two] got up and returned at once to Jerusalem. There they found the Eleven and those with them, assembled together and saying, "It is true! The Lord has risen and has appeared to Simon." Then the two told what had happened on the way, and how Jesus was recognized by them when he broke the bread.

While they were still talking about this, Jesus himself stood among them and said to them, "Peace be with you."

They were startled and frightened, thinking they saw a ghost. He said to them, "Why are you troubled, and why do doubts rise in your minds? Look at my hands and my feet. It is I myself! Touch me and see; a ghost does not have flesh and bones, as you see I have."

When he had said this, he showed them his hands and feet. And while they still did not believe it because of joy and amazement, he asked them, "Do you have anything here to eat?" They gave him a piece of broiled fish, and he took it and ate it in their presence.

He said to them, "This is what I told you while I was still with you: Everything must be fulfilled that is written about me in the Law of Moses, the Prophets and the Psalms."

Then he opened their minds so they could understand the Scriptures. He told them, "This is what is written: The Christ will suffer and rise from the dead the third day, and repentance and forgiveness of sins will be preached in his name to all nations."

Luke 24:33-47a

Jesus Christ was light against darkness, righteousness against rebellion, truth against deception, goodness against wickedness, life against death, hope against despair . . . and the glorious news is that He triumphed over every enemy and made our salvation sure.

HE ROSE

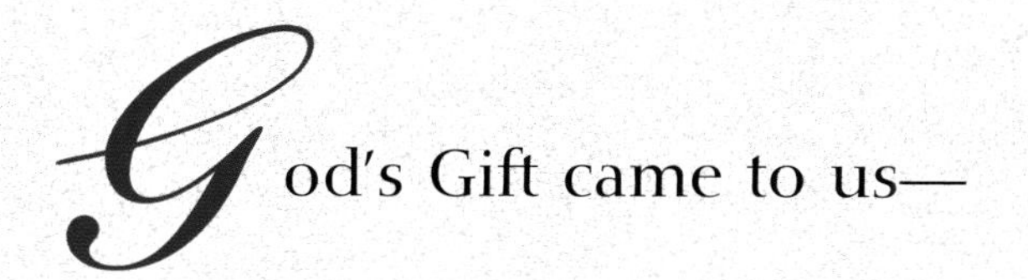

God's Gift came to us—

Not because we were good, but because we had sinned;

"all have sinned, and come short of the glory of God."

Romans 3:23 (KJV)

Not because we had it all together, but because we were lost;

"the Son of man is come to save that which was lost."

Matthew 18:11 (KJV)

Not because we loved Him, but because He first loved us.

"This is love: not that we loved God, but that he loved us and sent his Son as an atoning sacrifice for our sins."

I John 4:10

Where would we be without Jesus? He is all there is and all that really matters!

God loves us so much that He took on our humanity,
walked with us for awhile, spoke with, touched,
and ate with us. Laughed, cried, and shared our joy.
He knows us!
When He died and rose again, He did not leave us alone.
His comfort wraps us up, and His Spirit lives in our hearts.
Through Him we can become what we were meant to be.
He loves us!
What a Gift we've been given! The Gift of Christ will never
wear out or fade away. It will only grow richer, deeper,
stronger, and more precious.

He Rose

God knew we could never buy our way to Him—

the cost was too great.

We could never earn our way to Him—

the task was too great.

We could never will our way to Him—

the commitment was too great.

God knew we could never come to Him . . .

so He came to us!

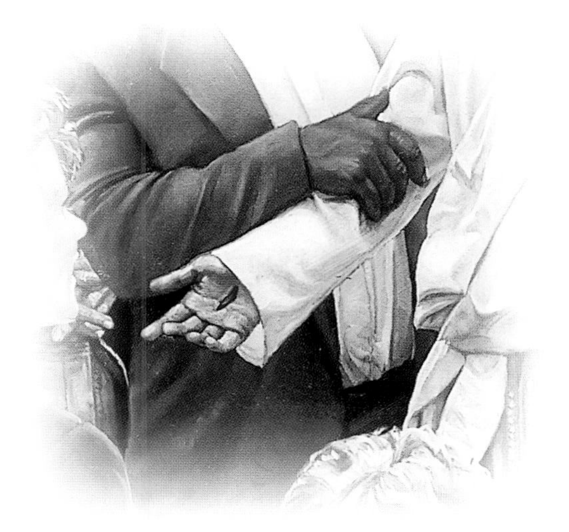

He took nothing with Him
as He left His Father and His home.
He put aside the glory
and the fellowship He'd known.
Every right of Deity
He gladly laid all down,
To walk as man among us,
and seek a different crown.
From the highest heaven
He sought redemption's plan,
As thorns were put upon His head,
and nails into His hands.
He was despised, rejected,
and faced the cross alone,
And when His work was finished,
He triumphantly went home.
Now He is with His Father,
seated by His side—
Planning out His wedding day
and waiting for His bride.

IMMANUEL—"GOD WITH US"

For the mother who seeks God's peace

in the midst of life's demands—

for the father who desires

to provide the right example—

for the child who wants

to grow in strength of character—

for the servant who wants

to be found faithful—

for the believer who wants

to be used to touch the lives of others—

God, in Christ, came and lived among us.

There is no better news than the words of the prophets . . .

no richer treasure than the pearl of great price . . .

no deeper joy than the light of His presence . . .

no greater gift than the life of God's Son . . .

There is no better way to live than

to have Jesus Christ at home in our hearts!

He Rose

Jesus Christ came, not to receive but to give . . .

not to be served but to serve . . .

not to please Himself

but to give His life as a ransom . . .

not to be a distant Savior,

but to be our closest friend!

When Jesus speaks to His own,

He never uses words of despair, hopelessness,

frustration, defeat, discouragement, fear,

confusion, or failure. Instead, He speaks

words of hope, rest, victory, assurance, peace,

power, joy, purpose, and love.

The Word of God became flesh,
the Son of God became a man,
the Lord of all became a servant,
the Righteous One was made sin,
the Eternal One tasted death,
the Risen One now lives in men,
the King of kings is coming again.

If there ever was a doubt,
the coming of Jesus Christ settles it forever . . .
God really does love you!

God so loved the world that He came to change it.
The change would come by changing the people in it.
The change would not be a political, environmental, or economic change; it would be a change of the heart.
The heart change would come by receiving a gift.
The gift did not come in fancy wrappings, nor was it hidden in an inaccessible palace of a wealthy magistrate. It would be available to anyone who was humble enough to receive it.
The gift lived among us.
The gift was love—God's love in the form of a man. Each person that welcomed and received Him knew the change that only His love could make.

I found that change. It came when I received God's gift, Jesus Christ. Since that time my heart has never been the same. It has become a place of peace instead of confusion, a place of joy instead of heaviness, a place of love instead of fear.

This gift of new life has been given for you. It is my prayer that today will be the time when you receive God's gift, Jesus Christ, into your life—as you do, He will fill your heart with the good things that will last forever.

Roy Lessin

But as many as received him, to them gave he power to become the sons of God, even to them that believe on his name.

John 1:12 (KJV)

ABOUT THE AUTHOR

ROY LESSIN is a co-founder of DaySpring Greeting Cards and has been the senior writer for over twenty-five years. He is a graduate of Bethany School of Missions, where he received his ordination. Before writing for DaySpring, he was director of Christian education in Oakland, California and served as a missionary in Mexico and Puerto Rico. Roy has written several books, including *Forgiven*.

ABOUT THE ARTIST

CHRIS HOPKINS has done work for such clients as National Football League, National Geographic, Columbia Pictures, NBC, Nike. His painting *Peace, Be Still* is part of the *MasterPeace Collection*. Through his gift, Chris has been able to share his faith with others including fellow Christian artists. Chris, his wife, Jan, and their four children reside in Everett, Washington overlooking Puget Sound.